Will Eaves

EXPOSED STAIRCASE

Rack Press

First published in a limited edition of 150 copies,
the first fifty numbered and signed by the author.

The author would like to thank the editors of the *New Statesman* and the *TLS*,
and the organisers of Outburst Queer Arts Festival, Belfast, for publishing
earlier versions of three poems in *Exposed Staircase*.

For Sophie Scott

Published in Wales by Rack Press,
The Old Manse, Broad Street, Presteigne Powys LD8 2AD
All orders and correspondence: rackpress@nicholasmurray.co.uk

ISBN 978-1-8382303-3-3

Printed by Artisan Print, Presteigne, Powys

Matinée

Behind the clouds it goes,
the clouds like scenery
trucked on by hidden hands
to wring great changes
out of light – the lessened
light of afternoons
in childless parks.
It's all so massive, dark
and miniature –
the street, the buildings
and the fungal sky like ink
or blood in an aquarium.
Where are the FX guys,
the ones who make me
want to believe my eyes?

Perfectly Good Legs

for Kristin Headlam

God didn't like his skinny legs
and made better ones for mankind from
red meat, collagen and calcium.
Just like that. Shorts followed.

Later, noticing
the way his creatures idolised
a certain thickness of thigh,
he tried to say – no,

no: that wasn't what I meant.
Love the sturdy. Do, please. Be
my guest: all I wanted was a chance
to stand on feet at a normal distance

from my hips, and walk
towards the unexplained cow
on a beach looking at her shadow.
Sometimes I think these things

up and then I'm stuck with them.
But he couldn't speak. It felt wrong.
He withdrew into the singing cloud
and measured his desolations.

Omen

After the wind stops,
  we are sloshed
to and fro in the silence
  like drowned ducklings

or a photograph developing
  in its tray.
Harder and harder to avoid,
  these images of aftermath

and no reply:
  a still garden
where the blossom
  neither fails nor fruits,

the seedlings never push up
  from the root,
the bee never docks
  in the colour-blind flower.

The Path

On the far side of the high bridge
stands a clump of willows
losing leaves
in the blank November lamplight.
The morning is all angles and degrees
like the coots practising lift-off
in their quarter of the pond
or the willows stopped
by nothing in the act of falling.
Two dark moons of mistletoe
in the treetops
lend themselves to the air of observation
and habit below:
half-inflated swans seeing off dogs,
a pair of crows discussing their arthritis,
people carried round the park
on a thin grey carousel.
Last leaves stencil the white horizon
with waders' feet
and the bridge is behind me.

The Nerd in Love

I don't want to be clever.
It's enough to look at the moon
with its yarmulke at an angle and say: "My feet are cold";
much better than cleverness, "as I have argued elsewhere"
or "as I have repeatedly emphasised" – phrases lit
with exhaustion and unintended comedy
like the faces of the prophets
and/or people who shout into dead microphones
at poorly attended demos.
Let's go inside.
The eclipse is over
and I want so much to show you
the full extent of my stupidity:
"a point not in doubt but about which I wish to be clear."

Asleep with flowers and TV

Beneath you is the swollen city,
markets and the plenaries of feral cats,
their siestas under siege from cops
with eyeshades up and windows down
tooling around in old Buicks.
There's a whiff of stock footage about
it – sex on the breath of my first lover
from the interior. After light rain,
elms take a stand in a foreign park.
They spread their arms, raise lantern
blossom against purple incoming.
The years have issued a new print
of our one film, which I watch daily,
never mind the slow wow you suffer
in playback, tailback, fanning out.

Before It Was Called Anything

Let it rain and let the parquet lack lustre.
Mark Humphrey, who grew up to be a physicist
and rogue among the many Mark Humphreys
who are not physicists, got ink
on his fingers and lower lip

to the exasperation of the teacher,
an extraordinary authority in those days –
and axiomatically our superior
in the matter of maths and charts.
Suppose Mark knew more

than he was letting on. When it was time
for home, we raided the coat-pegs
and possibly the sun
came out – let four bright windows stretch
across the floor to Mark's unbuckled feet.

Or suppose it didn't and he had no cause
to linger at his desk, distracted
by the herringbone wood,
chevrons found always to the right of "Play"
and the length of his socks. Let them also be a pair.

Poplars

On a chicane in the rapids
Walter drops from his canoe,
gets pulled into a narrow sluice
and sticks. His circling friends
discuss the matter of the rope:
"No worries, Walt. We'll get
a line out, figure something."
But the trapped boy has
already weighed the odds.
A cry could shake the others'
hands, the rope's tense thought.
Around him the loaned world,
his dog hot-footed on the far side
in a slow descent of sovereigns.

Cygnet

One dies in the egg but six are strong.
  An eighth slips feebly from the nest –
He falls onto his mother's back.
  She carries him around the pond

In a sort of gala spectacle:
  White feathers his sedan, for torches
Tall grass holding up the sun,
  The magpies and the grey heron.

Reverses

Candlelight makes a black double-yolk
of the lampshade on the ceiling, while wind,
at the glass, wants more from tired-parent
buildings than they can give. But come inside,
track down the hallway past a Dalí fence
of damp socks on the radiator, and you will
appreciate the heretofore as items, not working
things, far less reminders of love and overthrow.
(Aren't remains a shade duller for being so
composed? Ask piglet, out back, or the hens.)
Pale skies free up the post-industrial morning,
and, look, you find yourself on a newly exposed
staircase, which has nothing to transact: no
polished attribute or power of conveyance.

The Mad

Answers are pat.
They do not reach the mad
At the end of long tables.
They do not even reveal
Who makes such ugly tables.
Today the whole street
Is full of knowing, but silent
Like the inside of a mirror.
The neighbourhood felines,
Released from window duty,
Exchange frank looks that say
Without saying all they might:
If it's answers you're after,
Try better questions.